D1201329

CITIES OF THE WORLD

WASHINGTON, D.C.

BY R. CONRAD STEIN

CHILDREN'S PRESS®
A Division of Grolier Publishing
New York London Hong Kong Sydney
Danbury, Connecticut

CONSULTANTS

Professor Edward C. Smith
Director of American Studies & Special Assistant to the Dean
College of Arts and Sciences
American University, Washington, D.C.

Linda Cornwell
Coordinator of School Quality and Professional Improvement
Indiana State Teachers Association

Project Editor: Downing Publishing Services
Design Director: Karen Kohn & Associates, Ltd.
Photo Researcher: Jan Izzo

Visit Children's Press on the Internet at:
http://publishing.grolier.com

Library of Congress Cataloging-in-Publication Data
Stein, R. Conrad.
      Washington, D.C. / by R. Conrad Stein.
          p. cm. — (Cities of the world)
      Includes bibliographical references and index.
      Summary: Describes the history, culture, daily life, people, sports,
and points of interest in the capital of the United States.
      ISBN 0-516-21192-7 (lib. bdg.)   0-516-26532-6 (pbk.)
      1. Washington (D.C.)—Juvenile literature. I. Title.
II. Series: Cities of the world (New York, N.Y.)
F194.3.S72   1999   99-12387
975.3—dc21   CIP
                                          AC

GROLIER
PUBLISHING

TABLE OF CONTENTS

THE WASHINGTON MONUMENT

Rising grandly from the heart of Washington, D.C., stands the Washington Monument. Its lines are simple and clean. Some claim that the white marble obelisk looks like a giant candle. Despite its simplicity, the Washington Monument fills viewers with pride. Many people get goosebumps when they see this shrine to George Washington. In a city of monuments, it is clearly the most famous.

Washington, D.C., is the capital city of the United States. The D.C. stands for District of Columbia, a diamond-shaped segment of land administered by the U. S. Congress. Washington has close neighbors in Maryland and Virginia but is not part of any state. The city lies wholly within the District of Columbia.

The capital is one of the most visited cities in the world. Every year, from 20 to 35 million people from the United States and foreign countries come here. Tourists walk with wonder around the National Mall and gaze at the White House and the U.S. Capitol. They are thrilled by the incredible variety of Washington's museums. Few cities are as beautiful.

The Capitol at dusk

Friends on an outing

A *refrigerator magnet featuring the Washington Monument*

No other city in the United States gives tourists so many things to do and sights to see in such a compact space.

Some 4 million people live in Washington and its suburbs. The capital is an immensely friendly city that welcomes visitors. Most visitors begin their trip at the Washington Monument.

The Washington Momument, symbol of the nation's capital

The city of Washington has few industries. Instead, the government is by far the major employer. About one in every five workers in the metropolitan area hold government jobs. Washington has been called "the nation's biggest company town," with the federal government as the big boss.

INSIDE THE BELTWAY

Political writers like to say, "That's life inside the Beltway," or "How's that going to work inside the Beltway?" The Beltway (or the Capital Beltway) they speak of is Interstate 495, a superhighway that forms a ring around Washington's metropolitan area. The phrase "inside the Beltway" refers to the city of Washington and its nearby suburbs in Virginia and Maryland.

The suburban Beltway communities house people (mostly government workers) who hold jobs within the city. However, in recent years, many government agencies have moved to the suburbs. Thousands of men and women work in the offices of the National Institute of Health in Bethesda, Maryland, and at the Central Intelligence Agency in McLean, Virginia. The Pentagon, in Arlington, Virginia, is the largest office building in the world and is the daytime home for more than 20,000 office workers.

Profound differences hold sway between the city and its sea of suburbs. The city bears the stamp of history. Many of the city's residential neighborhoods are more than 100 years old. The suburbs, on the other hand, grew mostly after World War II. The capital's outlying communities look like modern suburbs anywhere in the nation.

Springtime in Chevy Chase

*Beautiful old homes
in Georgetown*

*A Washington
mail carrier
fills her cart.*

Since the 1950s, the population of Washington proper shrank while the suburbs saw a dramatic increase in their number of residents. By 1995, the city's population was 550,000, down one-fourth since 1970. At the same time, the suburbs mushroomed.

Many Washington neighborhoods are impoverished. A survey taken in 1996 reported that 22.3 per cent of Washington's city dwellers live below the poverty level. The impoverished communities, like other communities nationwide, suffer drug problems and have a failing school system. Therefore, when many working-class families acquire enough money, they flee the city to find a more pleasant lifestyle in the suburbs. Washington does have many excellent neighborhoods. Communities such as Georgetown and Dupont Circle have beautiful old homes, elegant shops, and safe streets. Other fine neighborhoods include Cleveland Park, Spring Valley, and Adams-Morgan.

Race is another factor that distinguishes the city of Washington from its suburbs. Washington is 65.8 percent black. Of all American cities, only Detroit, Michigan, and Atlanta, Georgia, have a larger proportion of African-American residents. By contrast, the majority of people living in the suburbs are white.

There is nothing new about the preponderance of African Americans living in the nation's capital city. For generations, blacks have moved to Washington seeking a better life for their families.

For many African Americans, Washington has proved to be a success story. A 1998 study said black families in Washington have a median annual income of $39,896, the highest such figure for African Americans of any city in the nation. The same study ranked Washington first in the number of black residents with a college degree, first in the percentage of black families earning more than $75,000 a year, and sixth in the percentage of black households that were homeowners.

A professional African-American couple poses with their two daughters.

Three children enjoying a carnival ride

Arlington National Cemetery

An estimated 4 million people a year visit the famous Arlington National Cemetery in the suburb of Arlington, Virginia. Two presidents, John F. Kennedy and William Howard Taft, are buried there, along with nearly 300,000 veterans of American wars. About 35 burials a week are conducted at Arlington. Also in the cemetery stands the Tomb of the Unknowns, which holds unknown soldiers who died in World War I, in World War II, and in the Korean War. The inscription on the Tomb of the Unknowns reads: HERE RESTS IN HONORED GLORY AN AMERICAN SOLDIER KNOWN BUT TO GOD.

BLACK WASHINGTON—A STUDY IN CONTRASTS

Edward Brooke was born in Washington in 1919. An African American, he lived in a mostly segregated neighborhood. Yet he has pleasant memories of the Northwest Washington of his childhood: "The houses were red-brick, identical three-story buildings attached in a row to each other. . . . Our neighborhood was quiet and friendly, and everyone knew just about everyone else." Brooke served in World War II and won a Silver Star for bravery. After the war, he graduated from Washington's Howard University. Brooke later moved to Massachusetts and in 1966 was elected a U.S. senator in that state. He was the first African American to be elected to the U.S. Senate in almost 100 years.

Brooke grew up in a middle-class Washington community. His father was a lawyer. His neighbors and his church urged young people to study hard and excel at work.

Senator Edward Brooke giving a speech in 1968

Marion Barry, Controversial Mayor

Marion Barry, a veteran civil-rights worker, was elected mayor of Washington in 1978. Barry demanded greater home rule for the city, and managed to anger many members of Congress. As mayor, he was never able to escape controversy. In 1991–92, Barry served six months in prison following a drug conviction. Yet many voters, especially those in the African-American community, remained loyal to Barry. Upon his release, he ran for mayor again and won. In 1998, Barry announced he would not seek reelection.

Cedric Jennings, an African-American teenager, wasn't raised with the opportunities afforded Edward Brooke. Jennings attended Washington's Frank W. Ballou High School in the 1990s. He was a gifted student, but his excellent grades made other students jealous of his abilities. They teased him, bullied him, and even beat him up. Jennings sometimes played hookey and deliberately failed tests to seek relief from his tormentors. His plight was written about in a 1998 book called *A Hope in the Unseen*. The book describes grim conditions in Washington's high schools, where some 40 percent of the students drop out

A Washington, D.C., couple with their five-year-old daughter

well before graduation. Cedric, however, through sheer intellect and willpower, overcame the obstacles in his path. He graduated from Ballou with straight As and went on to Brown University.

Washington lies in the southern region of the United States. Until the 1960s, many southern states had laws restricting the lives of African Americans. They were barred from eating in the same restaurants with whites, and they were forced to sit on the back seats of buses. Those segregationist practices were less stringent in Washington. Also, in the days before laws barred discrimination in hiring, the federal government was one of the few employers willing to hire blacks on an equal basis with whites. Therefore, blacks streamed into Washington seeking government jobs.

Yes, there are thousands of poor African Americans living in the capital, but few other cities have fostered such a strong African-American middle and upper class as has Washington, D.C.

A woman inspecting sheets of uncut money at the U.S. Mint in Washington

Junior-high-school friends sitting side by side

A STEPCHILD OF GOVERNMENT

In September 1997, the children of Washington's inner-city schools hurried to school to start their new semester. Upon arriving at school, they were turned away at the door. The reason? Many schools had leaking roofs that the city had failed to fix over the summer. A judge ordered the schools closed until the roofs could be repaired.

To the children and their families, this situation was nothing new. For the previous three years, school openings had been delayed because buildings were in need of repairs.

Washington has a peculiar relationship with government. Though it is administered by Congress, it has it own—weak—local government system. The local government cannot collect enough tax money to repair school buildings and maintain other city services.

For more than 100 years, the city of Washington has struggled to achieve "home rule." With home rule, Washingtonians would have the right to run their city in the same way urban residents do in the rest of the nation. Though Congress passed a Home Rule Charter for the city in 1973, it provides only for an elected mayor, a thirteen-member council, and a nonvoting delegate to the House of Representatives. Congress, however, has the authority to veto any legislation. Some powerful members of the U.S. Congress oppose expanded home rule. They do not want the city to have the power to elect voting delegates to Congress. At one time, Washington, D.C., mayors were appointed by

A girl with her chow puppy

the federal government instead of being elected by the people. Until 1964, Washingtonians were not even allowed to vote for president of the United States.

Washingtonians complain that their inability to achieve true home rule makes city financing difficult. About one-third of the city's funds come from the federal government. Most Washingtonians believe that Congress fails to allocate enough money to run the city properly.

That is the main reason the city has been unable to keep up with school building repairs. Critics say that Washington is not a child of the federal government, but a stepchild.

Washington is a city that tugs at American hearts. It is the focal point of national pride. The city has held this special place in the American spirit for nearly 200 years.

This late evening view shows the Potomac River, the Capitol, the Washington Monument, and the Lincoln Memorial.

A NATION

At the beginning of its history, the United States did not have a permanent capital. Philadelphia served as a temporary capital during the American War of Independence (1775–1783). George Washington took his oath of office in New York City, the temporary capital in 1789. Clearly, the nation needed a headquarters, a city to serve as a seat of government and as a place for common celebrations. The site for such a city was selected by the nation's first president. The capital was soon named after him.

BIRTH OF THE CAPITAL

On a June morning in 1791, George Washington rode a horse through a section of lovely land that sprawled over the states of Virginia and Maryland. The land lay in a **Y** formed by the Potomac and Anacostia Rivers. This raw, undeveloped spot was des-tined to be the capital city for the United States of America.

Riding with the president was Pierre Charles L'Enfant. Born in Paris, L'Enfant was an architect, an engineer, and a painter. President Washington appointed him to be the chief planner for the new city. The idea of creating a modern city out of bare ground thrilled L'Enfant. He dreamed of building a bold metropolis, one designed to inspire a new nation.

Washington and L'Enfant rode up what was locally called Jenkins Hill. L'Enfant later wrote that the hill stood "as a pedestal waiting for a monument." In the years to come, the hill got its monument. Beginning in 1793, the U.S. Capitol was built on its crest. The hill was soon called Capitol Hill.

President George Washington laying the cornerstone of the U.S. Capitol in 1793

L'Enfant envisioned broad tree-lined boulevards leading like spokes on a wheel toward Capitol Hill. With statues, fountains, and stately public buildings, Washington would rival any city in Europe.

But L'Enfant had an artistic temperament that clashed with politicians. He quarreled with government officials and with prominent landowners. Just one year after his appointment, L'Enfant was dismissed from his position. Work on the capital fell to Andrew Ellicott, who tried to preserve L'Enfant's grand vision. L'Enfant, a dejected man, died penniless. He is now buried on a hill in Arlington National Cemetery. From his grave, there is a marvelous view of the city of L'Enfant's dreams.

Pierre L'Enfant, architect and engineer, planned the city of Washington, D.C.

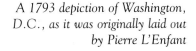

A 1793 depiction of Washington, D.C., as it was originally laid out by Pierre L'Enfant

It was not until 1800 that Washington officially became the capital city of the United States. That year, a train of horse-drawn wagons rolled over the country roads bringing in 126 government workers. John Adams, the nation's second president, moved into a still-incomplete building called the President's House. That building was later renamed the White House. Adams made a brief statement concerning the White House: "May none but honest and wise men ever rule under this roof."

The first residents of Washington were dismayed by what they saw. Workers' shacks lined the roads. Only one wing of the Capitol was finished. The President's House smelled of wet cement. Pennsylvania Avenue, the main street, was a muddy wagon path. Abigail Adams, the wife of President John Adams, wrote her daughter, "Woods are all you see from Baltimore until you reach the city, which is only so in name."

Those with vision, however, understood the future greatness of this place. Other cities grew like weeds in any direction. From the beginning, however, Washington had a central plan, based on the designs of Pierre L'Enfant. Over the years, the plan was changed and often neglected. Still, Washington remained unique. It is one of the world's few great cities that was designed before it was built.

John Adams (left), the second president of the United States, was the first to live in the President's House, later renamed the White House.

Below: A view of Pennsylvania Avenue as it looked in 1800

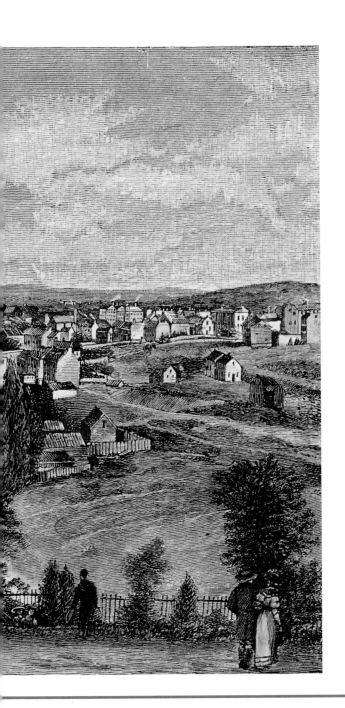

Benjamin Banneker, Mathematical Genius

Andrew Ellicott chose one of the country's top surveyors to lay out the streets of Washington. He was Benjamin Banneker (1731–1806), a free black man who had attended only a few months of formal school. Banneker had taught himself complex subjects such as calculus and trigonometry. He also built a remarkable wooden clock, carving each gear by hand. The clock kept perfect time for more than 50 years.

A 1980 commemorative stamp honoring Benjamin Banneker

WASHINGTON AT WAR

On August 24, 1814, panic swept Washington. At a nearby bridge, British troops routed an American force and were preparing to storm the capital. Roads swarmed with civilians fleeing from town.

One Washingtonian preparing to evacuate was Dolley Madison, wife of President James Madison.

Before leaving, she coolly packed many state papers and a splendid portrait of George Washington into a wagon. Then she, along with some 8,000 other Washingtonians, abandoned their city.

With drums beating and fifes playing, the British marched into the American capital. They found the streets almost deserted. Several officers entered the President's House and helped themselves to the food and wine that was still on the table. Troops broke into the Capitol and set it on fire. The nearby Treasury was also put to the torch. A wall of flames erupted and spread from building to building. Attorney General Richard Rush and President Madison looked down on the embattled capital from a nearby hill.

Later, Rush wrote, "Columns of flame and smoke ascended throughout the night. . . . The President's House and other public buildings were on fire, some burning

At the height of the War of 1812, the British set fire to Washington, D.C.

slowly, others with bursts of flame and smoke mounting high."

The burning of Washington took place at the height of the War of 1812. For Great Britain, the capture of Washington was a triumph. For the United States, the capital's destruction was one of the lowest points in the nation's history. After the war, the city of Washington was quickly rebuilt. It grew with the energy of the young nation.

But from the country's beginnings, its people were divided over the institution of slavery. President Thomas Jefferson, himself a slave owner, warned that slavery alarmed Americans like "a fire bell [ringing] in the night."

Slavery triggered the terrible American Civil War, which broke out in 1861. Wartime Washington became a base camp, crowded with troops. Thousands of runaway slaves also sought refuge in the city. The grounds at nearby Arlington were first

The White House and grounds about 1858, three years before the American Civil War began

used as a cemetery during the conflict. At war's end, Arlington already held 18,000 graves. Slavery was one of the main causes of the conflict, and freedom for the slaves was one of its final results. Once more, the city of Washington suffered war and endured.

A Union soldier of the Thirty-First Pennsylvania Infantry with his family near Fort Slocum, Washington, D.C.

THE PULSE OF THE NATION

In the late 1800s, government buildings and elegant apartment houses rose in the capital. A small canal called Tiber Creek was paved over to become Constitution Avenue. In 1902, railroad tracks and warehouses were cleared away to create the parklike Mall. Today, the Mall serves as a walkway for millions of tourists. Year by year, Washington developed as the country's special treasure.

The Capitol about 1886

This photograph of Pennsylvania Avenue was taken about 1900.

Washington also became a forum, a gathering place to express the nation's joys, sorrows, and anger. Freedom of speech is a right guaranteed to American citizens. Many people feel there is no better place to express that right than in Washington. Therefore, Washington has long been the site of protests, triumphs, tears, and music—all part of the American drama.

The Great Depression struck the country in the 1930s. One in four workers lost their jobs. Banks failed. Hardworking families were thrown out of their houses because they could not pay rent. Particularly angry were the veterans who had fought in World War I between 1917 and 1918. The veterans had been promised bonus money, but the depression-strapped Congress refused to grant them funds. In 1932, thousands of "bonus marchers" poured into Washington to demand their checks. The former servicemen clashed with regular army troops, who

In 1932, thousands of "bonus marchers"—veterans of World War I—came to Washington to demand the bonus checks they had been promised.

used tear gas to quell the protest.

A joyful protest took place in 1963. It was the height of the civil-rights era, when Congress was debating laws that would finally end discrimination against African Americans. On a beautiful sunlit August afternoon, more than 200,000 citizens joined the "March on Washington," to urge Congress to pass new civil-rights measures. Authorities feared that the March on Washington would erupt in a riot. Instead, a grand celebration prevailed. Perfect strangers— black and white—sang together and held hands. The highlight of the march came when Dr. Martin Luther King Jr. stood at the Lincoln Memorial and thrilled the crowd with a stirring speech that included the words: "I have a dream that one day this nation will rise up and live out the true meaning of its creed: 'We hold these truths to be self-evident; that all men are created equal.'"

Just three months after the March on Washington, President John F. Kennedy visited Dallas, Texas. Shots were fired at his motorcade and the president was killed. Kennedy, youthful and vigorous, had a way of reaching out to people and exciting them with hope. Americans adored his lovely wife and children. The entire nation wept as his funeral procession wound through Washington's streets on the route to his gravesite in Arlington National Cemetery.

The 1960s were years of unrest. The Vietnam War dragged on, taking thousands of young lives. Cities across the nation exploded in rage after Martin Luther King Jr. was gunned down by an assassin in April 1968. The worst rioting took place in Washington, where 10 people were killed and arsonists started some 700 fires. The army was called in to quell the riot. No Washingtonian who lived through those times will ever forget the shocking sight of machine guns emplaced on Pennsylvania Avenue.

A horse-drawn caisson bearing the body of assassinated President John F. Kennedy on its way to the Capitol on November 24, 1963.

The Wall of Healing

Stretching along a walkway near the Lincoln Memorial are two long, black granite walls. Many of the people who gather there weep as they study the walls. Inscribed on the granite face are almost 60,000 names. They represent the young men and women who died in the Vietnam War. That war divided the United States almost as badly as did the American Civil War. Officially, the wall is called the Vietnam Veterans Memorial. Erected in 1982, the memorial attempts to heal old wounds and reunite the country.

Washington remains at the center of the country's emotions. In the 1990s, groups such as the Million Man March (led by several African-American organizations) and the Promise Keepers (a Christian alliance) came to the city. AIDS awareness organizations held demonstrations there. The city has been a protest point for environmentalists, disability-rights activists, and dozens of other interest groups. The nation's pulse can always be felt in Washington, D.C.

Above: Washington, D.C., police fire tear gas to disperse rioters gathered to loot and start fires in reaction to the assassination of Dr. Martin Luther King Jr. in April 1968.

CAPITAL

Life in Washington is exciting. On holidays, parades wind through the streets and bands play in the parks. Entertainment is everywhere in this city. And much of the entertainment is public, free to all.

CELEBRATING AMERICA

There is no better place to spend the Fourth of July than in the nation's capital. Independence Day celebrations begin with a parade down Constitution Avenue. On the front steps of the National Archives building, a military band plays and a speaker reads the Declaration of Independence. Jazz festivals, arts-and-crafts shows, and food fairs are held throughout the city. In the evening, the National Symphony Orchestra gives a free concert outside the Capitol. To end the celebration, the night skies above the city explode with a dazzling display of fireworks.

Fourth of July fireworks exploding over the capital

Washington is above all a political town. Therefore, one of its most intense celebrations is held once every four years when the president is inaugurated. Inaugurations take place late in January. The ceremony begins at the Capitol, where the president takes the Oath of Office and makes a speech. Over the years, the speeches and the ceremonies have reflected the times. Abraham Lincoln was inaugurated in 1861, amid an atmosphere of hatred that would soon explode into the Civil War. Soldiers stood guard on the rooftops during Lincoln's inaugural parade because it was feared someone would try to assassinate the new president. Franklin Roosevelt's 1933 inaugural address was given during the Great Depression, when much of the nation was mired in poverty. Boldly, Roosevelt said, ". . . the only thing we have to fear is fear itself."

A paperweight featuring the Capitol of the United States of America

People of all ages enjoy the capital's Fourth of July celebrations.

35

Dozens of other fun and historic events dot the capital's calendar. Martin Luther King Jr.'s birthday is honored in January with speeches and music at the Martin Luther King Jr. Memorial Library. In March, the Cherry Blossom Festival celebrates the blooming of the city's famous Japanese cherry trees. Also in March, the Smithsonian Institution holds its annual Kite Festival on the Washington Monument grounds. The White House Easter Egg Roll is a fun-filled party for small children. The National Frisbee Festival is held in September at the Washington Monument. Veterans Day, in November, honors the nation's war dead with a wreath-laying ceremony at Arlington National Cemetery. Every December 5, the president flicks a switch and launches the Christmas season at the National Tree-Lighting Party.

Children and parents around a bunny pole during the annual Easter Egg Roll on the White House lawn

The annual Kite Festival is held on the Washington Monument grounds across from the Lincoln Memorial.

Easter eggs like these (and those on the opposite page) are used in the annual White House Easter Egg Roll.

The Marine Band, a Washington Institution

Experts claim the Marine Band, stationed in Washington, is the best marching band in the world. The band has played at inaugural parades for every president since Thomas Jefferson's first administration in 1801. The Marine Band consists of 148 men and women who parade in bright red coats. From 1880 to 1892, Washington-born John Philip Sousa (who is buried in the city's famous Congressional Cemetery) led the Marine Band. Known as the "March King," Sousa wrote many beloved patriotic songs, including "The Stars and Stripes Forever" and "El Capitan."

THE SPORTING LIFE

In Northwest Washington sprawls the popular Rock Creek Park. Covering 1,754 acres (710 hectares), the park is Washington's favorite playground. It is also the city's gymnasium. A 4-mile- (6.4-kilometer-) long bicycle path runs along Rock Creek. The park's sidewalks serve as raceways for skateboarders and in-line skaters. Joggers pound the streets. Hikers explore Rock Creek's rugged landscape and see an occasional deer or fox.

Washington is a sports-crazy city. Bicycles are everywhere. They are even allowed on the city's subway trains. Boating is popular on the Potomac River. Outdoor basketball courts in inner-city neighborhoods are always crowded with children. The city has about 150 tennis courts, and all have long lines of people waiting their turn to play.

Residents of Washington wildly support their local teams, such as pro football's Washington Redskins. Fans still admire Redskin heroes of the past—John Riggins, Doug Williams, and Mark Rypien. Pro basketball's Washington Wizards enjoy a loyal following. The Washington Capitals are the delight of hockey lovers. High school and college basketball teams have strong support. Many Washingtonians consider the Georgetown University Hoyas to be the darlings of college basketball competition.

In this very political city, the nicknames of teams can stir controversy. Many critics believe the name "Redskins" dishonors Native Americans. In 1997, the pro basketball team changed its name from the Bullets to the Wizards.

Washington Redskins quarterback Doug Williams making a play during the 1988 Super Bowl

The Washington Capitals
play professional hockey.

Washington has no baseball team of its own. Baseball fans follow the Orioles who play for the nearby city of Baltimore, Maryland. But in years past, Washington had its own baseball squad, and the Washington Senators were the most-talked-about sports team in the capital. Often, however, the Senators had dismal seasons. When the Senators played poorly, a joke was told in the capital's night clubs: "Washington: first in war, first in peace, and last in the American League."

Many Washingtonians follow the
Georgetown University Hoyas basketball
team (left) with great enthusiasm.

THE WONDERFUL WORLD OF THE SMITHSONIAN

In 1829, a very wealthy British scientist named James Smithson died. He left an unusual will. Smithson ordered that his fortune go to Washington, D.C., to establish a museum in that city. Smithson had never in his life visited the United States. Why he gave such a generous grant to Washington, D.C., is a mystery to this day. The money arrived in 105 bags containing some 100,000 gold coins. Its value totaled about $500,000. At the time, the money in those bags made up one of the largest single fortunes on earth. Smithson asked only that the museum be called the Smithsonian Institution.

Above: A stamp commemorating the Smithsonian Institution
Below: The National Gallery of Art is part of the Smithsonian complex.

The Smithsonian Institution is now the largest museum complex in the world. It has fourteen museum buildings and galleries in Washington, D.C. The institution also sponsors the National Gallery of Art and the National Zoological Park. Its most popular museum buildings stand along the Mall in the heart of the capital city. All the Smithsonian museums along the National Mall are free. Guests need only walk in the front doors.

Walk the Mall today and take in an exciting museum experience. Start with the National Air and Space Museum, the most visited of all the Smithsonian museums. At the entrance are aircraft that make up the Milestones of Flight exhibit. Prominent among them is the 1903 kitelike airplane that took Orville Wright on the first powered flight ever achieved by a human being. Below the Wright brothers' airplane is the spacecraft that carried men to the moon just 66 years later. Also in the building is a flat rock taken from the surface of the moon. Go ahead, touch it. The moon rock is one of many "hands-on" exhibits at the National Air and Space Museum.

A souvenir arm patch from the National Air and Space Museum

The Wright brothers' airplane that made the first power-driven flight in 1903 is exhibited in the National Air and Space Museum. Below it is the Apollo spacecraft that carried men to the moon in 1969.

Next door to the Air and Space Museum is the Hirshhorn Museum and Sculpture Garden, where some 2,000 sculptures thrill art lovers. At the outdoor garden, the modern American sculptures appear to be dancing to unheard music. The huge National Museum of Natural History displays fossils millions of years old and ferocious-looking dinosaurs. Also in the Natural History Museum is the enchanting Hope Diamond, the most famous gem in the world. The National Museum of American History contains 16 million objects, including old postage stamps and coins. Displayed there is the 1813 flag that inspired Francis Scott Key to write "The Star-Spangled Banner."

Stroll the Mall to the other Smithsonian attractions. The Castle, the first Smithsonian building, opened in 1852. Tour the National Museum of Art, the National Museum of African Art, and the Freer Gallery of Art. As you enter these wonderful museum buildings, thank Mr. Smithson, that mysterious Englishman, for his long-ago gift to a country he had never seen.

The Castle was the first Smithsonian building to be erected.

A magnet showing the Castle

One of the most popular exhibits in the National Museum of Natural History (above) is the famous Hope Diamond.

The Holocaust Museum

Washington has dozens of museums other than those sponsored by the Smithsonian Institution. The most moving is the United States Holocaust Memorial Museum, opened in 1993. This museum tells the tragic story of the World War II years when millions of Jews, Gypsies, and the physically and mentally disabled were put to death by the Nazi government in Europe. Haunting family photos and personal items such as watches and eyeglasses belonging to those who died are displayed. Touring the Holocaust Museum is an experience with a message: Never again can civilization stand silently and allow mass murder to take place.

CAPITAL

Washington, D.C., is one of the most walkable cities in the United States. Many of its monuments, historic buildings, and other treasures can best be seen on foot. A proper tour of the capital takes days or even weeks. But visitors with limited time can concentrate their sight-seeing on the section between Capitol Hill and the Lincoln Memorial. This is historic Washington, the pride of the nation. And this whole area can be seen in one long, glorious walk.

THE CAPITOL NEIGHBORHOOD

The great dome of the Capitol rises 300 feet (92 meters). On its top stands the bronze *Statue of Freedom*. The magnificent dome was added during the Civil War. The Capitol is the place where the U.S. Congress meets. Its interior serves as a museum, with statues, wall carvings, paintings, and delicate furniture. In many respects, the building is a grand American palace.

Near the Capitol stands the Library of Congress Building. Founded in 1800, it now holds the largest library collection in the world. Its main reading room is crowned by a dome made from marble of three distinct colors. Displayed in the Library of Congress are many national treasures. The rough draft of the Declaration of Independence, handwritten by Thomas Jefferson, is there. Also shown is Pierre L'Enfant's original design for the city of Washington.

The bronze Statue of Freedom *stands on top of the Capitol dome.*

Right: Union Station

Below: An overview of the main reading room in the Library of Congress

The Union Station Story

In the old days, most travelers to Washington arrived by train. In 1907, the city opened the ornate Union Station near Capitol Hill. At the time, it was the world's biggest railroad station. Built with sweeping arches and colossal statues, it was a terminal designed to thrill travelers with its own beauty. But trains soon lost favor to car and airplane travel and the little-used station was allowed to deteriorate. In 1986, the city launched a $160-million project to restore the station to its former greatness. Today, some 60,000 people a day pass through Union Station. In addition to serving travelers, the building houses an inviting array of restaurants, shops, and movie theaters.

The highest court in the land meets at the Supreme Court Building. Visitors are advised to come on Monday, when the nine justices take their seats on the bench to hand down decisions. Over the years, the Supreme Court has changed the American way of life with landmark measures such as outlawing racial segregation in schools and ensuring equal rights for women. The building itself is made from dazzling white Vermont marble and looks like a Greek temple. Carvings on its massive doors trace the history of justice from ancient to modern times.

Left: Stamps commemorating the Statue of Freedom, which stands atop the Capitol dome, and the United States Supreme Court Building
Below: The Supreme Court Building

Children enjoying a hands-on exhibit at the Capital Children's Museum

The National Postal Museum houses rare stamps (below), post-cards, and personal letters.

Two interesting museums stand in the Capitol Hill neighborhood. The National Postal Museum, opened in 1993, is the newest Smithsonian museum building. Among the approximately 16 million items housed there are rare stamps, postcards, and personal letters. In the main hallway are 70-year-old airplanes that were once used to carry the mail. The Capital Children's Museum is a learning playground designed for children from two to twelve. The theme here is to learn by doing. Children study cultures of other lands by trying on furs from Russia and eating tacos typical of those made in Mexico.

NORTH OF THE NATIONAL MALL

A massive limestone build-ing on Pennsylvania Avenue houses the National Archives. This is a fascinat-ing storehouse holding his-toric papers, photographs, and other items dating to the country's beginnings. In Exhibition Hall of the National Archives build-ing are the nation's three most precious docu-ments: the original Declaration of Independence, the Constitution, and the Bill of Rights. The Archives' library holds haunting pho-tographs, many from before the Civil War. In all, more than 9 million historical pictures are stored at the National Archives.

A replica of the Declaration of Independence

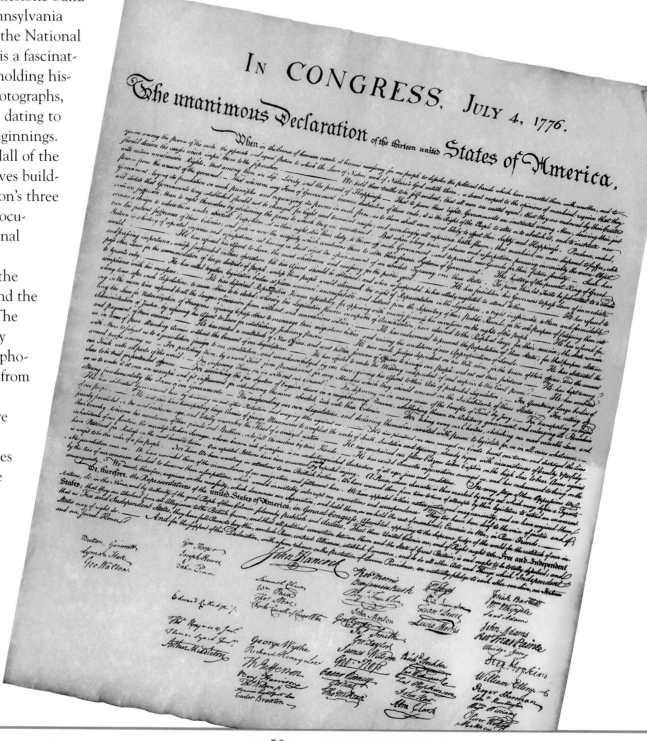

It is sometimes called "The Strongbox for the Nation."

Pennsylvania Avenue is the path of presidents and the scene of historical drama. Inaugural parades march down Pennsylvania Avenue from the Capitol. Solemn processions marking state funerals use the avenue. Over the years, soldiers celebrating victory parades at the end of wars have paraded down Pennsylvania Avenue amid cheering crowds. In many respects, Pennsylvania Avenue is America's Main Street.

The Metro

Our tour in this book is confined to one lengthy but entertaining walk. However, if you wish to commute from neighborhood to neighborhood or to the suburbs, you should take the city's Metro. The mostly underground subway system runs 89 miles (143 km) and is still expanding. Its 74 stations are clean, well-lit, and attractive. The streets of the capital are often congested with car traffic, making the Metro the best way to get around.

Left: A young Hispanic Washingtonian

Easily the most important address on Pennsylvania Avenue is 1600, the White House. Every U.S. president except George Washington has lived there. The White House is open daily for guided tours, but expect to wait in line. Guests are led past the famous 1797 portrait of George Washington that Dolley Madison rescued from the rampaging British army. In all, the White House has 132 rooms. Five rooms—the Blue Room, East Room, Red Room, Green Room, and State Dining Room—are open to the public. The Blue Room has ornate furniture, some of which is covered with gold leaf. Hanging in the Red Room are stunning paintings by renowned American artists such as Gilbert Stuart and Albert Bierstadt.

Walk south from the White House and cross the Ellipse, a 52-acre (21-ha) oval park. Every December, the president lights the National Christmas Tree on the Ellipse while carolers sing and bands play. The nearby Bureau of Engraving and Printing offers guided tours so guests can see the fascinating process of how the country designs and prints its paper money.

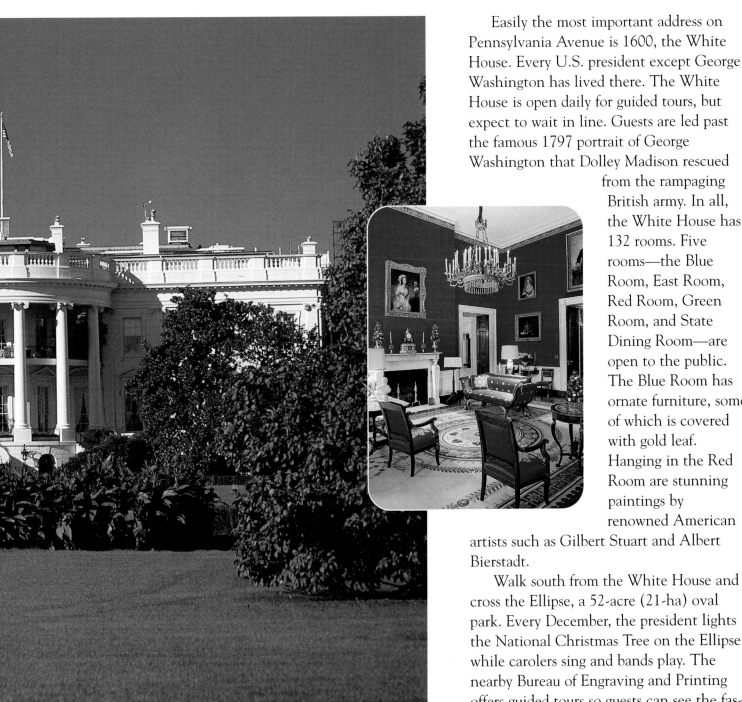

Above: A view of the White House from the South Lawn
Inset: The Red Room

COMPLETING YOUR WALK

The Corcoran Gallery of Art is one of the capital's finest art museums. The museum holds paintings by such masters as Rembrandt, Turner, and Degas. Near the Vietnam Veterans Memorial stands the Vietnam Women's Memorial. This special tribute to the estimated 10,000 women who served in Vietnam shows statues of three nurses tending a badly wounded soldier. The Korean Veterans Memorial displays life-sized statues of 19 soldiers marching cautiously, as if they were on a combat patrol.

Opened in 1997, the Franklin Delano Roosevelt Memorial occupies 7.5 acres (3 ha) and includes statues, waterfalls, and gardens. Displays highlight aspects of Roosevelt's four elected terms as president.

Below: The Jefferson Memorial
Right: A medal depicting the Jefferson Memorial during the Cherry Blossom Festival

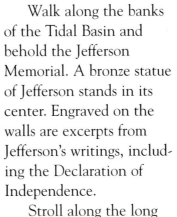

Walk along the banks of the Tidal Basin and behold the Jefferson Memorial. A bronze statue of Jefferson stands in its center. Engraved on the walls are excerpts from Jefferson's writings, including the Declaration of Independence.

Stroll along the long and narrow Reflecting Pool. Its water is designed to act as a mirror and reflect both the Lincoln Memorial and the Washington Monument. Feel the drama of history as you walk. At this site, thousands of cheering people heard Martin Luther King Jr. tell of his dream. Just a few years later, angry crowds gathered here to denounce the Vietnam War. The American right of free speech has made these remarkable grounds an open-air forum.

Brooding over the Reflecting Pool is the Lincoln Memorial with a seated statue of Abraham Lincoln. Some say he looks lost in sad thoughts. Others claim they see a slight smile on his face. Dedicated in 1922, the Lincoln Memorial is the anchor of the Mall.

Stand with your back toward the Lincoln Memorial, facing the Washington Monument. Observe the Capitol dome rising in the distance. Gaze down and capture the image of the Washington Monument framed beautifully in the Reflecting Pool. This is a Washington sight that will live forever in your memory. The city awes foreign visitors and instills pride in all Americans. More than just a capital, Washington is the soul of the nation.

Above left: The statue of President Abraham Lincoln in the Lincoln Memorial

Left: A youngster poses on the statue of FDR's Scottie dog Fala at the Franklin Delano Roosevelt Memorial

FAMOUS LANDMARKS

The American Red Cross Building

*Right: The Kennedy Center for the Performing Arts
Below: The National Arboretum*

The Washington National Cathedral

The sixth-largest cathedral in the world, this monumental building has been described as a "Gothic masterpiece." Work began on the twin-towered structure in 1907, and was not completed until 1990. Funeral services for Presidents Wilson and Eisenhower were held here. President Woodrow Wilson is buried in the cathedral grounds, making him the only president whose grave lies within the city limits.

National Zoological Park

One of the most entertaining zoos in the country, it is home to more than 3,000 animals. The zoo lies in a scenic gorge cut by Rock Creek. Founded in 1889, it is administered by the Smithsonian Institution.

Georgetown University

Established in 1789, Georgetown is the oldest Catholic university in the country. More than 6,000 students attend the school, and its basketball teams are followed by many Washington sports fans. The university is the focal point of the Georgetown neighborhood, one of the finest residential areas in the capital city.

Dupont Circle and Embassy Row

Dupont Circle is a green island in the midst of tall buildings and swirling traffic. Washingtonians play chess or talk politics while sitting on its benches. Nearby is Embassy Row, a line of historic mansions on Massachusetts Avenue that are now embassies for dozens of countries.

John F. Kennedy Center for the Performing Arts

Completed in 1971, the Kennedy Center is the cultural heart of the capital city. Concerts, plays, and films are presented here. The building is home to the National Symphony Orchestra and the Washington Opera.

The Boy Scout Memorial

This is a "must see" for visiting Boy Scout troops. Near Lafayette Square, the memorial shows the bronze statue of a Boy Scout.

The Watergate Complex

Called a "city within a city," the Watergate is a series of high-rise buildings that house a hotel, offices, apartments, and many shops and restaurants. With sweeping curves, the buildings are a city landmark. But the Watergate Hotel will always be remembered for a 1972 burglary of the Democratic Party's headquarters. Nixon re-election campaign workers and others were later connected to the burglary, and the scandal forced President Richard Nixon to resign his office in 1974.

Far left: Georgetown University
Left: The U.S. Marine Memorial, known as the Iwo Jima Statue
Above: The Watergate Complex

The Potomac River

The city's most prominent natural feature, the river is spanned by graceful bridges such as the Francis Scott Key Memorial Bridge, the Theodore Roosevelt Memorial Bridge, and the Arlington Memorial Bridge. Its waters feed the Washington Channel and the Tidal Basin. During the Civil War, the Potomac separated the Union from the Confederate States.

Marine Corps Memorial

Popularly known as the Iwo Jima Statue, the monument commemorates the 1945 battle for the Japanese-held island of Iwo Jima. After landing on the island's beaches, the Marines fought their bloodiest battle so far in the Pacific campaign. At the top of Iwo Jima's highest mountain, four Marines raised a flag and a photographer snapped a dramatic picture. The picture thrilled the country and was later immortalized in this great statue.

Arlington House

Rising over Arlington National Cemetery is this stately house once owned by Confederate general Robert E. Lee. The house and its furniture accurately reflect Lee's time. Thousands of visitors tour Arlington House each day.

The National Arboretum

Southwest of Capitol Hill spreads the U.S. National Arboretum. It is a 440-acre (178-ha) plot of gardens and woods. More than 10,000 species of plants grow here. In the spring and summer, thousands of azaleas and exotic plants such as Siberian larch and Manchurian lilac bloom on the arboretum's grounds.

Navy Museum

This museum houses ship models and items used by the U.S. Navy since its founding in 1794. Particularly interesting to young guests are World War II anti-aircraft guns that a visitor can sit in and pretend to be firing at enemy airplanes.

The American Red Cross Building

The national headquarters of the famous Red Cross organization is also an architectural gem. A gleaming white structure, it features Tiffany stained-glass windows.

The Pentagon

The headquarters of the American military forces, the Pentagon is also the world's largest office building. It has 17 miles (27 km) of hallways and 284 rest rooms. Enough telephone wire is strung through its walls to wrap around the earth two and a half times.

FAST FACTS

POPULATION (1990)

City:	606,900
Metropolitan Area:	4,223,485

AREA City: 68 square miles (176 sq km)
Metropolitan Area: 6,511 square miles (16,863 sq km).
The city of Washington, D.C., lies wholly within the section of land called the District of Columbia; it is the only American city that is not part of any state.

CLIMATE The average July temperature is 78 degrees Fahrenheit (26° Celsius); the average January temperature is 37 degrees Fahrenheit (3° Celsius). Summers can be uncomfortably humid. By contrast, Washington can experience spells of bitter cold during the winter.

President Ronald Reagan's second inaugural parade (January 20, 1985) had to be canceled because temperatures and wind-chill factors plunged well below zero degrees Fahrenheit (–18° Celsius).

INDUSTRIES Government is by far the biggest employer for Washington and its metropolitan area. An estimated one in every five workers in Washington and the suburbs hold government jobs. Publishing is a relatively large industry, as several national magazines and two major newspapers are headquartered in the capital. Scattered factories in the metropolitan area produce food products and nonelectrical machinery.

CHRONOLOGY

1751
The city of Georgetown is established; Georgetown is now a prominent Washington, D.C., neighborhood.

1788
Both Virginia and Maryland offer land for a future capital city.

1791
Congress authorizes President George Washington to choose a site for a new capital city. Washington selects the present site and appoints Pierre L'Enfant to design the capital.

1793
George Washington lays the cornerstone of the Capitol.

1800
Washington officially becomes the capital of the United States. John Adams (the second president) moves into the newly completed President's House, later called the White House.

1814
British troops loot the city and burn important buildings including the Capitol and the White House during the War of 1812.

1829
James Smithson, a British scientist, dies and leaves an unusual will. Smithson gives a large fortune to the U.S. government to establish a museum in Washington. He stipulates that the museum be called the Smithsonian

Institution. Today, the Smithsonian Institution is the largest museum complex in the world.

1861
Abraham Lincoln is sworn in as president, and the Civil War breaks out just five weeks later. During the war, the city's population swells with troops and with runaway slaves.

1865
The Civil War ends and Lincoln is assassinated at Ford's Theatre in Washington.

Rock Creek Park

1867
Howard University, the city's first African-American university, is chartered.

1885
The Washington Monument is completed.

1890
Rock Creek Park and Potomac Park are established; the city's population reaches 230,000.

1922
The Lincoln Memorial is dedicated.

1932
Thousands of World War I veterans join a "bonus march" on Washington, and an ugly riot ensues.

1935
The Supreme Court Building is completed.

1943
The Jefferson Memorial is dedicated.

1963
The "March on Washington," headed by Martin Luther King Jr., attracts thousands of peaceful demonstrators.

1968
Race riots rock the city after Martin Luther King Jr. is assassinated in Memphis, Tennessee.

1973
Congress passes a limited home rule measure that allows Washington residents to elect their own public officials, including their mayor.

1982
Work is completed on the Vietnam Veterans Memorial.

1997
The Franklin D. Roosevelt Memorial is dedicated.

WASHINGTON, D.C.

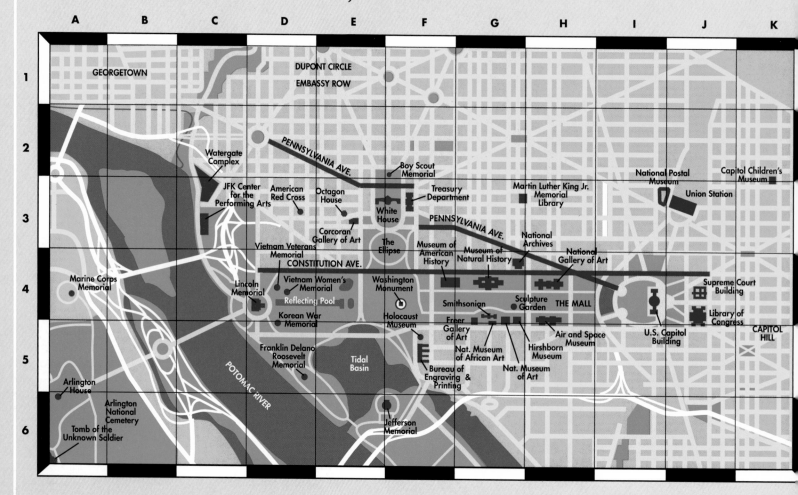

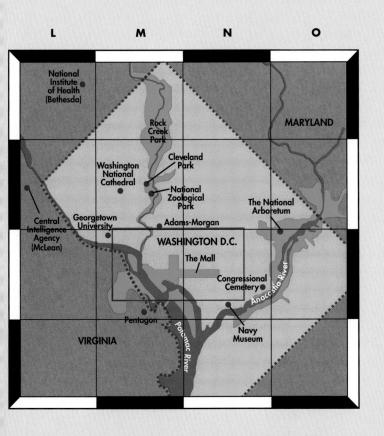

WASHINGTON, D.C. & SURROUNDINGS

GLOSSARY

alliance: A group with a common cause or goal

fife: A flutelike instrument commonly played by military bands

forum: A place where one is invited to speak and state one's beliefs on matters

fostered: Nourished or promoted

median: The middle value in a series of numbers

obelisk: A tall, tapered, four-sided stone pillar with a pyramid-shaped cap

plight: A difficult or dangerous condition or journey

preponderance: The most common item or the strongest item in a series

quell: To put an end to

stringent: Strict, rigid

temperament: A condition of one's personality

Picture Identifications

Cover: The U.S. Capitol as seen from the Capitol Reflecting Pool; a mother and daughter
Page 1: Children with face painting of U.S. flag
Pages 4-5: The Washington Monument as seen from the Tidal Basin
Pages 8-9: Students at George Washington University
Pages 20-21: The White House in 1877
Pages 32-33: Japanese girls in native dress hold cherry blossom sprigs during the Cherry Blossom Festival
Page 33: A Cherry Blossom Festival stamp
Pages 44-45: The U.S. Capitol

Photo Credits ©

NDEX

TO FIND OUT MORE

BOOKS

Ashabranner, Brent K. *A Memorial for Mr. Lincoln*. New York: G. P. Putnam's Sons, 1992.

Brill, Marlene Targ. *Building the Capital City*. Cornerstones of Freedom series. Chicago: Childrens Press, 1996.

Butler, Brian. *D.C. for Free: Hundreds of Free Things To Do in Washington, D.C.* Memphis, Tenn.: Mustang Publishing, 1994.

Doherty, Craig A. *The Washington Monument*. Woodbridge, Conn.: Blackbirch Press, 1995.

Donnelly, Judy. *A Wall of Names: The Story of the Vietnam Veterans Memorial*. New York: Random House, 1991.

Fradin, Dennis Brindell. *Washington, D.C.* From Sea to Shining Sea series. Chicago: Childrens Press, 1992.

Guzzetti, Paula. *The White House*. Parsippany, N.J.: Dillon Press, 1996.

Hilton, Suzanne. *A Capital Capital City, 1790–1814*. New York: Atheneum, 1992.

Kummer, Patricia K. *Washington, D.C.* One Nation series. Mankato, Minn.: Capstone Press, 1998.

Pedersen, Anne. *Kidding around Washington, D.C.: A Young Person's Guide*. Santa Fe: John Muir Publications, 1993.

Peduzzi, Kelli. *Shaping a President: Sculpting for the Roosevelt Memorial*. Brookfield, Conn.: Millbrook Press, 1997.

Rubin, Beth. *Washington, D.C., with Kids*. A Frommer's Family Travel Guide. New York: Macmillan Travel, 1996.

Santella, Andrew. *The Capitol*. Cornerstones of Freedom series. Chicago: Childrens Press, 1995.

ONLINE SITES

Franklin Delano Roosevelt Memorial
http://www.nps.gov/fdrm/index2.htm
A description of the FDR Memorial, which was dedicated in 1997, with links to the outdoor rooms and sculptures in the memorial, the inscriptions, waterfalls, gardens, shade trees, and more; also includes links to the FDR Library, FDR Home, Eleanor Roosevelt Home, and Campobello International Park.

A Guide to Washington, D.C.
http://www.physics.georgetown.edu/Wash.html
Information on just about everything you ever wanted to know about Washington, D.C., including numerous links to local information such as newspapers, theater, dance, fun and recreation, a parents page, a dining guide, news and weather, museums and parks, Georgetown sports, professional sports, the White House,

Congress, the Supreme Court, goverment servers, universities and colleges, libraries, and more.

Georgetown University
http://www.georgetown.edu/
This guide to the university includes information on academic programs; admissions & financial aid; libraries; research & technology; news & information; student life & services for law-center students, medical-center students, under-graduates, graduate students; and much more.

United States Capitol
http://www.aoc.gov/homepage.htm
An information resource developed and maintained by the Architect of the Capitol; includes links to the construction history, architectural features, and historic spaces; works of art; the Capitol grounds; the Congressional Office Building; the U.S. Botanic Garden; and more.

Welcome to Arlington County, Virginia
http://www.arlingtoncounty.com/Default.htm
This site provides information on all aspects of the county, including general information, parks and recreation, Arlington Cemetery, and more.

Washington, D.C. Travel Packet
http://washington-dc.travelpackets.com/
Save time and money by sending for this informative visitors travel packet that contains more than fifty brochures, maps, and discount coupons for your Washington, D.C., trip.

White House
http://www.whitehouse.gov/WH/Welcome.html
Information about the current president and vice president; White House history and tours; biographies of past presidents and their families; a tour of the historic building, current events; and much more.

ABOUT THE AUTHOR

R. Conrad Stein was born in Chicago. After serving in the U.S. Marines, he attended the University of Illinois where he earned a degree in history. He later studied in Mexico. Mr. Stein has published more than eighty history and geography books for young readers. He lives in Chicago with his wife and their daughter, Janna.